GLASS FROGS

DOUG WECHSLER

THE ACADEMY OF NATURAL SCIENCES

The Rosen Publishing Group's
PowerKids Press™
New York

For Michael and Patricia Fogden, whose work has been a great inspiration to me

About the Author
Wildlife biologist, ornithologist, and photographer Doug Wechsler has studied birds, snakes, frogs, and other wildlife around the world. Doug Wechsler works at The Academy of Natural Sciences of Philadelphia, a natural history museum. As part of his job, he travels to rain forests and remote parts of the world to take pictures of birds. He has taken part in expeditions to Ecuador, the Philippines, Borneo, Cuba, Cameroon, and many other countries.

Published in 2002 by The Rosen Publishing Group, Inc.
29 East 21st Street, New York, NY 10010

First Edition

Book Design: Michael de Guzman, Emily Muschinske

Project Editor: Kathy Campbell

Photo Credits: Page 11 (reticulated glass frog) © Michael Fogden/Animals Animals; all other photographs © Doug Wechsler.

pp. 4, 8, 15, 22 (inset) Glass frog (no common name), (*Cochranella mydas*); pp. 7, 12 Emerald glass frog (*Centrolene prosoblepon*); p. 11 Reticulated glass frog (*Hyalinobatrachium valerioi*); p. 16 Ctenid spider (*Cupiennius coccineus*); p. 19 Pacific giant glass frog (*Centrolene geckoiddeum*); p. 20 Glass frog (species not identified).

Wechsler, Doug.
Glass frogs / Doug Wechsler.
     p. cm. — (Really wild life of frogs)
Includes bibliographical references (p.   ).
  ISBN 0-8239-5857-4 (lib. bdg.)
1. Glass frogs (Amphibians)—Juvenile literature. [1. Glass frogs (Amphibians) 2. Frogs.] I. Title.
  QL668.E23 W43 2002
  597.8'7—dc21
                                                            2001001117

CONTENTS

DOUG SAYS

THERE ARE AT LEAST 74 SPECIES OF GLASS FROGS IN THE COUNTRY OF COLOMBIA, SOUTH AMERICA.

EMERALD FROGS

A tiny, emerald green frog with green bones sits on a green leaf. The leaf hangs over a rushing stream in a rain forest. It is night, and the frog calls with a high-pitched "creek creek creek." Meet the glass frog, one of the small wonders of the frog world. Glass frogs live along streams in Central America and South America. The glass frog **family** of frogs includes more than 100 **species**. All glass frogs are green, but each is a little different from the next. Once you know what one looks like, the rest will seem familiar. Why are they called glass frogs? The skin on the bellies of many glass frogs is **transparent**. This see-through skin gives these frogs their name.

Most glass frogs are small, usually about 1 inch (25 mm) long. The Pacific giant glass frog, though, can be 3 inches (76 mm) long.

TRANSPARENT TUMMIES

You may get a surprise when you look at the belly of a glass frog. The surprise is that you can see right through the skin. In some glass frogs, it is the skin of the chest that is clear. You can see the liver and can watch the heart beat. In another group of glass frogs, you can look straight through the skin and even through the walls of the gut. You can see even the food inside the gut. The third group does not have transparent skin, but you can see through the skin well enough to tell that the bones are green. Scientists do not know why glass frogs' guts are on display.

You can see through the skin of this emerald glass frog's underside. You can see also the dark food inside its gut.

KEEP OFF MY SPOT

During the rainy season, male glass frogs start calling from leaves over streams. Each species of glass frog has its own call. Some species make short, shrill whistles. Other species' calls are peeps or "ticks." A **herpetologist** who studies glass frogs does not have to see one to tell which species is calling. The herpetologist can tell each species of glass frog by its voice. A male glass frog's call tells other male glass frogs to keep off his spot on a leaf. It also attracts females who are ready to **mate**.

Each male defends his spot over the stream from other males. This spot is called his **territory**. If another male comes onto the leaf of the territory owner, the owner will jump on the **intruder**. Then the intruder usually struggles free and goes away.

The territory that a male glass frog defends is very small. It is about the size of one or two leaves.

EGGS ON LEAVES

Glass frogs mate and the female lays the eggs in the male's territory. The female lays from 20 to 30 eggs on the leaf. The leaf that carries the eggs hangs over the stream. After laying the eggs, the female leaves. The male usually watches over the eggs.

The male **reticulated** glass frog guards the eggs in his territory day and night. He protects the eggs from insects that might eat them. He also keeps the eggs from drying out by putting water on them. He gets the water by soaking it up through his skin. The water ends up in the frog's **bladder**. Then he urinates on the eggs to wet them.

A male reticulated glass frog guards eggs on the underside of a leaf over a stream. He protects the eggs from insects that might eat them.

BURIED TADPOLES

After the eggs are laid, big changes take place inside them. The round insides of each egg slowly change into a skinny tadpole. This takes about two weeks. The tadpole is ready then to come out, but it waits for rain. When it rains, the tadpole wriggles free of the egg and drops into the stream. If it lands on the ground by mistake, a flick of its powerful tail flips it back into the stream.

The glass frog tadpole buries itself in the leaves at the bottom of the stream. Its long tail helps it move through the leaves and **silt**. The tadpole has clear skin. The skin looks red because it has many **blood vessels**. These blood vessels soak up **oxygen** from the water and let tadpoles breathe through their skin.

An emerald glass frog climbs a tree. Glass frog tadpoles are hard to find. Scientists have never seen most kinds of glass frog tadpoles.

TO FIND A GLASS FROG

A stream in a wet, tropical **cloud forest** is a good place to look for glass frogs. Some scientists go to these forests to study glass frogs. Getting there can be a great challenge. In most parts of Central America and South America, it can mean camping out in a soggy place. Then the scientists must go out at night, when the frogs are active. It is best to wear a headlamp, a flashlight that is strapped to the head. The headlamp lets the scientists keep their hands free for balance when climbing up steep slopes. It seems very dark and lonely along a rushing stream at night. Seeing the glass frogs makes up for that. The scientists must search above and below leaves over the stream and listen for the frogs' high-pitched calls.

The sight of a glass frog will reward the scientist who returns to this stream at night with a headlamp.

ENEMIES

Glass frogs have the usual frog enemies, such as birds, snakes, and larger frogs, that like to eat them. Smaller animals also hunt the tiny glass frogs. **Ctenid spiders** hunt without webs. These spiders use their legs to grab glass frogs. The spiders kill the frogs with poisonous bites.

Many animals also eat glass frog eggs. Small crabs that live in the forest climb in the bushes in search of food. They crawl to the ends of leaves to munch on glass frog eggs. The crabs' hind legs hold onto leaves while their claws open eggs one at a time. The crabs eat the eggs and unhatched tadpoles. Wasps and flies also feed on the eggs.

Ctenid spiders like to hunt glass frogs for tasty meals.

PACIFIC GIANT GLASS FROG

Imagine you are creeping up a rocky stream in the Andes of western Ecuador. It is dark and mysterious. You work hard to push past bamboo and scramble over boulders. The songs of a hundred crickets ring in your ears. Suddenly your flashlight shines on a large, weird-looking frog. Its green skin has a bumpy texture. Its **webbed** toes have huge pads at the tips. Funny tabs stick out near its shoulders. This bizarre frog is a Pacific giant glass frog. The Pacific giant glass frog stands out among glass frogs. It is twice the weight of the second-largest species of glass frogs. It spends much of its time on rocks instead of leaves. Unlike most other glass frogs, it lays its eggs on rocks over streams instead of on leaves.

The Pacific giant glass frog has toe pads that help it to climb and cling to rocks, branches, and leaves.

CALLING ALL SCIENTISTS

Glass frogs in the mountains of Costa Rica seem to be in trouble. Like many frogs around the world, they are becoming hard to find. Scientists fear something is killing the frogs, but they do not know what. In Monteverde, Costa Rica, several other frogs have also become scarce or have disappeared. Golden toads are gone forever. Harlequin toads can no longer be seen there. It might take years of study by herpetologists and other scientists to find out why so many frogs are disappearing. The changing weather seems to be part of the problem. A **fungus** is also killing some frogs. Are we changing the **environment** in a way that hurts them? You might become a scientist someday and might help solve this problem.

Frogs have disappeared in many parts of the world. Scientists are trying to learn what is killing the frogs.

GLASS FROG DISCOVERIES

Scientists are still discovering new species of glass frogs. In 1960, scientists knew of only 23 species of glass frogs. Since then, about 87 more have been discovered, mostly in the countries of Colombia and Ecuador. No one has found more kinds of glass frogs than Dr. John D. Lynch. He started his studies looking for another group of frogs, called rain frogs. Dr. Lynch found many glass frogs, too. He decided to focus his search on glass frogs. He said, "So few glass frogs were known to scientists because too few people had explored cloud forests of Colombia and Ecuador at night. I was fortunate to be among the first scientists to see these beautiful frogs." Being a herpetologist can be pretty exciting.

GLOSSARY

bladder (BLA-der) The part of the body that stores urine.

blood vessels (BLUD VEH-suhlz) Narrow tubes, in the body, through which blood flows.

cloud forest (KLOWD FOHR-est) A very wet forest in tropical mountains that is often in the clouds.

Ctenid spiders (TE-nid SPY-derz) Tropical spiders with two or three leg claws.

environment (en-VY-urn-ment) All the living things and conditions that make up a place.

family (FAM-lee) The scientific name of a large group of plants or animals that are alike in some ways.

fungus (FUN-gis) A mushroom, mold, mildew, or related living things.

herpetologist (her-puh-TAH-leh-jist) A scientist who studies amphibians and reptiles.

intruder (in-TROOD-er) Someone or something that goes into a place without being invited.

mate (MAYT) When a male and a female join together to make babies.

oxygen (AHK-sih-jin) A gas in the air, which has no color, taste, or odor and which is necessary for people and animals to breathe.

reticulated (reh-TIH-kyoo-layt-ed) Having a pattern that looks like a net.

silt (SILT) Fine bits of earth, smaller than sand grains, found at the bottom of lakes and streams.

species (SPEE-sheez) A single kind of plant or animal. For example, all people are one species.

territory (TEHR-uh-tohr-ee) Land or space protected by an animal for its use.

transparent (tranz-PAYR-ent) Able to be seen through, sheer.

webbed (WEBD) Having skin between the toes as do ducks, frogs, and other animals that swim.

INDEX

WEB SITES

To learn more about glass frogs, check out these Web sites:
www.animalsoftherainforest.org/glassfrog.htm
www.zo.utexas.edu/research/salientia/centrolenidae/centrolenidae.html